ISBN 978-0-282-30731-8
PIBN 10847012

English
Français
Deutsche
Italiano
Español
Português

www.forgottenbooks.com

Mythology Photography **Fiction**
Fishing Christianity **Art** Cooking
Essays Buddhism Freemasonry
Medicine **Biology** Music **Ancient
Egypt** Evolution Carpentry Physics
Dance Geology **Mathematics** Fitness
Shakespeare **Folklore** Yoga Marketing
Confidence Immortality Biographies
Poetry **Psychology** Witchcraft
Electronics Chemistry History **Law**
Accounting **Philosophy** Anthropology
Alchemy Drama Quantum Mechanics
Atheism Sexual Health **Ancient History**
Entrepreneurship Languages Sport
Paleontology Needlework Islam
Metaphysics Investment Archaeology
Parenting Statistics Criminology
Motivational

Protecting Sherman's Lifeline

The Battles of Brices Cross Roads
and Tupelo 1864

by Edwin C. Bearss

Office of Publications
National Park Service
U. S. DEPARTMENT OF THE INTERIOR
Washington, D.C. 1971

The spring and summer of 1864 found the attention of the people of the North and South focused on the fighting in Virginia and Georgia. In these States, mighty armies fought battles that were to decide whether the United States was to be one nation or two. Interwoven with and having important repercussions on the fighting in Georgia were military operations in northeast Mississippi designed to prevent a Confederate cavalry corps under Gen. Nathan Bedford Forrest from striking into Middle Tennessee and destroying the single-track railroad over which Gen. William T. Sherman's armies drew their supplies. The Battles of Brices Cross Roads and Tupelo were fought to protect that railroad.

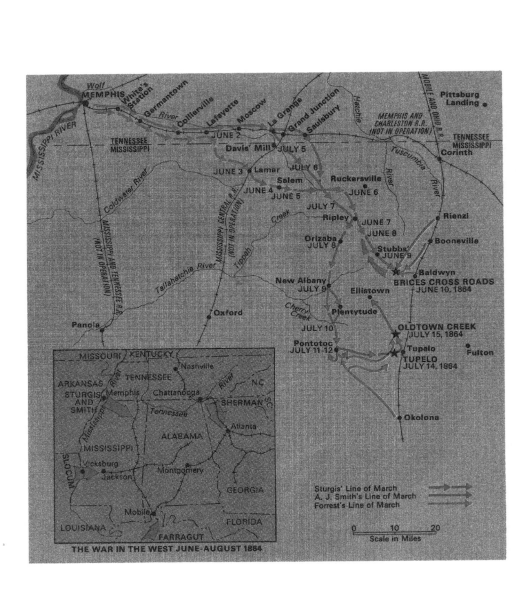

THE WAR IN THE WEST JUNE-AUGUST 1864

By the spring of 1864 almost 3 years of bloodshed and heartbreak had passed since the firing on Fort Sumter signaled the beginning of the Civil War, and the terrible fratricidal struggle continued with few signs of abatement. In the West, an army led by Gen. Ulysses S. Grant, supported by the Navy, had won a series of victories and had forced the surrender of Vicksburg in July 1863. The fall of Port Hudson a few days later gave Union forces control of the Mississippi River and divided the Confederacy. At Missionary Ridge, in the fourth week of November 1863, armies under Grant had driven the Confederates from the approaches to Chattanooga and recovered the initiative that had belonged to the South in that region since the Battle of Chickamauga in September. But in the east, Gen. Robert E. Lee's Army of Northern Virginia, despite its costly defeat at Gettysburg, remained a powerful fighting machine and guarded the approaches to Richmond.

Because of Grant's successes in the west, President Abraham Lincoln brought him east and in March 1864 gave him command of all United States armies. Vowing to defeat the Southern Confederacy, Grant proposed to employ the North's superior resources to grind it down in a war of attrition. The cost would be high, but the North could replace its losses while the South could not. In his planning, there was one factor that Grant could not overlook: if the major Confederate armies were still in the field in November, the electorate might send the Lincoln administration down to defeat at the polls. It was therefore crucial that Northern armies by November either defeat the South or score sweeping successes. A stalemate would be as bad a blow as a defeat.

Grant proposed to concentrate all his efforts on the

destruction of the two major Confederate armies and thus end the long, drawn-out war. He would personally oversee the movements of the forces whose goal was the defeat of General Lee's Army of Northern Virginia, maintaining his headquarters with the Army of the Potomac. In the west, Gen. William T. Sherman, who had succeeded Grant as commander of the Military Division of the Mississippi, was ordered to destroy Gen. Joseph E. Johnston's Army of Tennessee.

On May 5, 1864, coordinating his movements with Grant's, Sherman put his armies in motion through the pine-clad hills of northwestern Georgia, skillfully employing his superior numbers to outflank successive Confederate positions and compelling Johnston to fall back again and again. But by May 25 the Federal advance had been checked, for the time being, in front of New Hope Church. Although he had thrust deeply into Confederate territory, Sherman had failed to defeat Johnston, as the Southern leader gave up ground to gain time. Sherman's troops battled their way forward, their supply lines lengthening and becoming increasingly vulnerable to Confederate cavalry raids.

There were few cavalry leaders, North or South, whom Sherman respected; one was Nathan Bedford Forrest. A self-made man, Forrest had entered Confederate service as a private, and by repeated demonstrations of personal bravery, leadership, and audacity, he had risen to the rank of major general.

Holding little respect for soldiers who fought by the book, Forrest attributed his many successes to the simple fact that he "got there first with the most men." Powerfully built, he was ready to engage personally the

Nathan Bedford Forr
Bold and tenacious, a
fighter and a born lea
of men, he was admir
by military men bot
North and South. Wi
T. Sherman, Forrest
principal protagonis
called him "the most
markable man our ci
war produced on eith
side. . . . He alway
seemed to know what
was doing or intende
do, while . . . I could
tell or form any satis
tory idea of what he
trying to accomplish.

_Michael D. Brown

foe or to thrash any of his own men found malingering. No other American general has killed as many enemies with his own hand or has been wounded as often. His words of command as he led a charge were "Forward, men, and mix with 'em!"

Concurrently, Forrest led a cavalry corps based in northeast Mississippi. His corps was effective because he used it as mounted infantry. The men rode horses and mules to the scene of action, but Forrest usually made them fight on foot. Unlike most cavalry units, his men worked hard and could wreck a railroad as efficiently as Sherman's infantry. As Sherman's supply line lengthened, the Federal commander feared that "that devil Forrest" would get into Middle Tennessee and break the railroads behind him.

When General Forrest was in West Tennessee in March and April, Sherman telegraphed Gen. Cadwallader C. Washburn, the commander in Memphis, not to disturb the Confederate cavalryman, because he could do less harm by "cavorting over the country" there than elsewhere. Grant, however, could see that Forrest was recruiting his command while harassing and destroying isolated Union garrisons, and he directed Sherman to send enough troops to Memphis to chase Forrest back into Mississippi.

The first task was to find an officer equal to the challenge. Gen. Samuel D. Sturgis, a graduate of the U.S. Military Academy and an "old army" man, was chosen. A veteran of Wilson's Creek where he won promotion for "gallant and meritorious conduct," Sturgis had also served in the Army of the Potomac. In the winter of 1863–64, he had been commended for his cavalry leadership in East Tennessee. He had a chance to test Forrest

Samuel D. Sturgis. W Point graduate and M ican War veteran, Stu had a reputation as a lant and self-confide soldier. After the defe at Brices Cross Roads court of inquiry was c to look into the "disas and investigate claims he was intoxicated du the battle. No charg were ever filed agai Sturgis, but he finishe the war "awaiting ord

in the first week of May, as the Federals cleared the Confederates out of West Tennessee. His column, however, moved too slowly and the Southerners outdistanced it. Reporting to his superiors on May 7, Sturgis wrote: "It was with the greatest reluctance that I resolved to abandon the chase. Although we could not catch the scoundrel we are at least rid of him."

As Sherman's armies pressed deeper into Georgia, General Johnston knew that the only way to stop their advance was to destroy the Federal supply line—the railroad from Nashville and Chattanooga. Accordingly, he appealed to Gen. Stephen D. Lee for help in breaking the line.

Lee, a graduate of the U.S. Military Academy, commanded the Department of Alabama, Mississippi, and East Louisiana. Destined at 30 to be the Confederacy's youngest lieutenant general, his dark hair, beard, and eyes gave him a cavalier look. He had been present when the first shot was fired at Fort Sumter and had served as an artillerist in the Army of Northern Virginia until after the Battle of Antietam in September 1862. He had then been transferred to the west and led an infantry brigade in Gen. John C. Pemberton's army at Vicksburg. After Pemberton's surrender in July 1863, Lee was exchanged and placed in command of all the cavalry in Mississippi. He had assumed responsibility for the Department in May 1864 after the previous commander, Gen. Leonidas Polk, joined Johnston for the Georgia campaign.

Responding to Johnston's plea, Lee ordered Forrest and his cavalry to advance into Middle Tennessee and wreck the Nashville & Chattanooga Railroad. Forrest moved promptly. On June 1, he rode out of Tupelo,

Miss., with 2,000 specially chosen horsemen and a battery of artillery. Three days later, at Russellville in north Alabama, Forrest was overtaken by a courier with a message from S. D. Lee reporting that a powerful Union column had left Memphis to invade Mississippi. Forrest was told to forget the Middle Tennessee raid and return to Tupelo.

The Federals who had left Memphis were commanded by General Sturgis. They had been sent out by General Washburn in response to a call from Sherman to send a formidable expedition toward Tupelo, or in whatever direction Forrest happened to be. Sturgis' force, which moved out on June 1, mustered 4,800 infantry, 3,300 cavalry, 400 artillerists with 22 cannon, and a large supply train. The little army was organized into two divisions—one of infantry, the other cavalry. Gen. Benjamin H. Grierson, a former music teacher from Jacksonville, Ill., and now one of the North's best cavalrymen, led Sturgis' horse soldiers, many of whom were armed with seven-shot Spencer carbines.

Sturgis was to strike the Mobile & Ohio Railroad at or near Corinth and destroy any force that might be posted there. He then was to proceed down the railroad, wreck it, at least as far as Okolona, and return to Memphis by way of Grenada. Forrest's corps, during this sweep, would be dispersed and destroyed, and the countryside devastated.

On June 3, at Lamar, Sturgis' scouts told him that the Confederates had evacuated Corinth and retired down the railroad. Sturgis changed his line of march to intersect the railroad farther south. On the 4th, General Grierson, who had the lead, sent 400 of his horse soldiers racing eastward to Rienzi. The Federals reached the railroad, but before they could do much damage some of Forrest's men turned and drove them off.

Heavy rains pelted Sturgis' column as it bore southeastward through an area that had been ravaged by 2 years of raids and counter-raids. It was June 7 before Sturgis' infantry reached Ripley, 75 miles from Memphis. During the day, one of Grierson's brigades reconnoitered the New Albany Road and encountered a roadblock manned by two regiments sent out by Forrest to feel for the Federals. In the meantime, Sturgis advanced down Guntown Road. By nightfall on the 9th his command was concentrated and camped on Stubbs' farm, 9 miles northeast of Brices Cross Roads.

Forrest had returned to Tupelo from the aborted Middle Tennessee raid on June 6. Told about the general direction of Sturgis' march and that the Federals had broken the railroad at Rienzi, Forrest ordered two brigades to that point. Col. Tyree Bell's Tennessee brigade stopped at Rienzi, while Col. Edward Rucker's continued on, scouting for Sturgis toward New Albany. Forrest, with his artillery and escort, took position at Booneville, where he was joined by Rucker on the evening of June 9. Forrest also had two brigades at Baldwyn.

Gen. S. D. Lee reached Booneville on the 9th and went immediately to Forrest's headquarters for a briefing. After examining Forrest's troop returns and learning that his force numbered about 4,900 cavalry and 12 cannon, he suggested that Forrest retire toward Okolona and let Sturgis push deeper into Mississippi and farther from his base before giving him battle. Forrest was to move out on June 10 in the direction of Brices Cross Roads and then on toward Okolona. S. D. Lee, accompanied by two batteries of artillery, boarded a southbound train for Okolona.

That evening, June 9, Forrest called a number of his officers together. He told them that his spies had reported the Federals were encamped at Stubbs' farm, and that while he would prefer to get them into the open country where he could "get a good look at them," as Gen. S. D. Lee desired, the Confederates might be drawn into a battle before that could be realized. Orders were issued for the brigade and artillery commanders to have their men ready to ride before daylight and to push forward as rapidly as possible toward Brices Cross Roads.

Torrential rains, which did not cease until after midnight, turned the roads into ribbons of mud. When the sun rose, many knew that it would be one of those hot humid days which saps a man's vigor. As Forrest traveled with Rucker's brigade, he told Rucker he intended to attack Sturgis at Brices Cross Roads and outlined his battle plan:

I know they greatly outnumber the troops I have at hand, but the road along which they will march is narrow and muddy; they will make slow progress. The country is densely wooded and the undergrowth so heavy that when we strike them they will not know how few men we have. Their cavalry will move out ahead of the infantry, and should reach the crossroads three hours in advance. We can whip their cavalry in that time. As soon as the fight opens they will send back to have the infantry hurried up. It is going to be as hot as hell, and coming on a run for five or six miles over such roads, their infantry will be so tired out we will ride right over them.

Forrest then pushed ahead to join his advance brigade of Kentuckians commanded by Col. Hylan B. Lyon, an officer described by a Federal general as "a very rude and overbearing character."

Unlike the Confederates, the Federals did not make an early start on June 10. It was 5:30 a.m. before Grierson's horse soldiers swung into their saddles and started down Guntown Road; it was 7 o'clock before the infantry marched.

Grierson's vanguard encountered, charged, and scattered enemy pickets guarding the narrow bridge across Tishomingo Creek. By 9:45 the Union cavalry held Brices Cross Roads, and one brigade had followed the retreating Confederates 1 mile along Baldwyn Road. At the edge of a field, the Federals reined up their horses when they sighted Lyon's vanguard on the opposite side of the field, 400 yards away. While two of his companies charged the surprised Yanks, Lyon dismounted and deployed his 800-man brigade. Grierson did likewise, forming his 3,200 horse soldiers to the left and right of the road. Like the Confederates, most of the Federals fought on foot.

Forrest knew that he would have to gain and hold the initiative, or the "bulge," as he called it. Lyon's Kentuckians were advanced. For almost an hour, the Confederates drove forward, then retired, and advanced again. A great quantity of powder was burned and a few men killed or wounded, but General Grierson, unfortunately for the Union, had allowed himself to be bluffed by an inferior force.

Rucker's brigade now came up on a trot and formed on Lyon's left. Once again, Forrest waved his men forward. There was the sharp crack of small arms and the roar of artillery as the Confederates moved forward. On Forrest's left one of his battalions advanced too far and was sent reeling. Another brigade arrived, and Forrest posted it on Lyon's right. As soon as the troopers had

*y branch of the mil-
*y service is feverish,
*turous and exciting,
*e Cavalry. . . . there
*no music like that of
bugle, and no mono-
*o full of meaning as
link of sabres, rising
*lling with the dash-
*ce. Horse and rider
*ome one . . . and the
*ge, the stroke, the
*t of the carbines are
*quick, vehement and
*atic that we seem to
*atching the joust of
*aments or following
*Saladin and Crusad-
ers again."*

A. Townsend, Civil War
newspaper correspondent

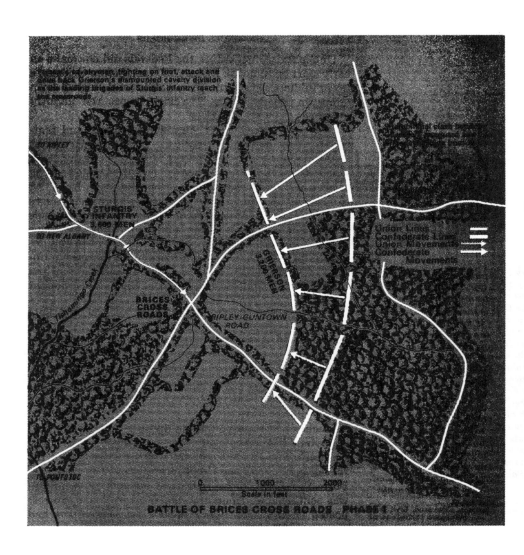

BATTLE OF BRICES CROSS ROADS, PHASE I

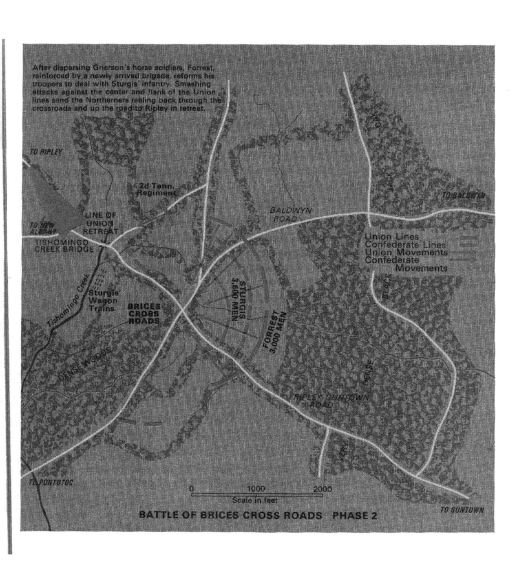

After dispersing Grierson's horse soldiers, Forrest, reinforced by a newly arrived brigade, reforms his troopers to deal with Sturgis' infantry. Smashing attacks against the center and flank of the Union lines send the Northerners reeling back through the crossroads and up the road to Ripley in retreat.

TO RIPLEY

2d Tenn. Regiment

BALDWYN ROAD

LINE OF UNION RETREAT

TO NEW ALBANY

TISHOMINGO CREEK BRIDGE

Tishomingo Creek

Sturgis' Wagon Trains

BRICES CROSS ROADS

STURGIS 3,500 MEN

FORREST 3,000 MEN

DENSE WOODS

RIPLEY GUNTOWN ROAD

TO SALDWYN

Union Lines
Confederate Lines
Union Movements
Confederate Movements

TO PONTOTOC

0   1000   2000
Scale in feet

BATTLE OF BRICES CROSS ROADS   PHASE 2

TO GUNTOWN

dismounted, they feigned an attack on Grierson's left.

It was now 11 o'clock, and, although Bell's brigade and the artillery had not reached the front, Forrest decided to assault Grierson. He rode along his line and encouraged his men, telling them that he expected everyone to move forward when the signal was given. At the sound of the bugle, the dismounted cavalry stormed across the field toward the Federals. Grierson's men held their ground and blazed away. At one point, Rucker's brigade penetrated Grierson's line, but the Federals called up two reserve regiments to close the breach. As the Yanks rushed forward, Rucker shouted for his men to draw "their six-shooters and close with them hand-to-hand." (Each man in Forrest's corps was armed with a rifle-musket and two Colt's revolvers. Forrest refused to arm his enlisted men with sabers, because he considered them useless in the type of fighting he favored.) After a desperate struggle, the Federals were forced to retire closer to Brices Cross Roads. By 12:30 Forrest had whipped Grierson's cavalry.

Grierson, on encountering the enemy, had sent a courier galloping to tell Sturgis that he had found the Confederates and needed help. As Forrest brought up fresh units and increased the pressure, Grierson repeated his plea for reinforcements with greater urgency. It was noon before Sturgis reached the field and after 1 p.m. before the advance columns of his infantry arrived though they had marched as fast as road and weather conditions would permit. They had tramped 9 miles since 7 o'clock; the "last three miles had been made at a trot, and the final mile at a double-quick."

The 3,600 infantry and their three supporting batteries filed into position covering the crossroads, their

"I need hardly add t
it is with feelings of t
most profound pain a
regret that I find my
called upon to record
defeat and the loss a
suffering incident to
verse at a point so fa
tant from the base
supplies and re-enfor
ments. Yet there is s
consolation in know
that the army foug
nobly while it did fig
and only yielded to c
whelming numbers."

Gen. Samuel D. Sturgis

left extending well north of Baldwyn Road and their right anchored about 200 yards west of Guntown Road. Between the crossroads and the Tishomingo Creek bridge was Col. Edward Bouton's black reserve brigade and the army's trains. Covered by the infantry, Grierson sought to re-form his exhausted division.

Colonel Bell's Tennessee brigade and Capt. John W. Morton's artillery now came up. The Confederate cannoneers, having traveled 18 miles, rode up at a trot, threw their eight guns into battery, and hammered away at Sturgis' masses with telling effect. The Union artillerists replied. Placing himself at the head of Bell's brigade, Forrest rode to the left, dismounted, and formed the newcomers. While Forrest was positioning Bell, the fighting ebbed. The only sounds were the occasional crack of a sharpshooter's rifle-musket, the rustle of underbrush as men moved about, and the hushed commands of officers. The weather was stifling—there was not a cloud in the sky and the air was still. Several men had been felled by sunstroke.

Forrest attacked. Because of the thick undergrowth covering most of the area, the Confederates were able to close to within a few paces of Sturgis' infantry. A crashing volley, however, sent part of Bell's battleline reeling back. The Federals called for a charge. Forrest's sixth sense had placed him at the key-point. As he dismounted, he shouted for his escort to do likewise. Accompanied by these daring fighters and with revolver in hand, he rushed the Federals. Additional men came up, and the counterattack was repulsed. In the hand-to-hand fighting, the bayonet of the Union infantry was no match for the heavy Colt's revolvers. The center of Sturgis' line crumbled, while the Confederate brigades on the right doubled back the Union left upon Ripley Road.

Off to the northwest in the direction of Tishomingo Creek, the 2d Tennessee Regiment, sent out by Colonel Bell to attack Sturgis' left and rear, had reached its objective "just as the fighting seemed heaviest in front." To deceive the Federals about their strength, the Confederates made a great commotion and a bugler galloped up and down the line sounding the charge. Not only did this show of force throw Sturgis' reserve brigade and the train guard into confusion, but Grierson sent off most of his cavalry to check the advance of the 2d Tennessee.

Forrest knew that the crisis had come, and that now the battle must be won or lost. Riding along behind his line, he told his troops that the enemy was starting to give way and that another charge would win the day. He told his young chief of artillery, Captain Morton, to be ready to advance four of his guns, double-shotted with canister, to within pistol range of the Federals at the crossroads. When the bugle sounded, the Confederate battleline pressed forward. At the same time, Morton's cannoneers drove their teams up the narrow country road. At point-blank range, they unlimbered their pieces and fired double-shotted canister into Sturgis' infantry with frightful effect. After a brief but savage fight, the Federals were routed from the crossroads, with the loss of three cannon.

General Sturgis grimly described this phase of the fight:

I now endeavered to get hold of the colored brigade which formed the guard of the wagon train. While traversing the short distance to where the head of that brigade should be found, the mainline began to give way at various points. Order soon gave way to confusion, and confusion to panic. The army drifted *toward the rear and was beyond control. The road became crowded and jammed with troops, wagons and artillery sank into the deep mud and became inextricable. No power could check the panic-stricken mass as it swept towards the rear.*

Several regiments, among them the 55th and 59th U.S. Colored Troops, attempted to check the onrushing Confederates; but assailed on the flanks, with Morton's guns sweeping their front with double-shotted canister, the Northerners broke. To add to the Federals' embarrassment, a fleeing teamster's wagon overturned on the narrow wooden bridge over rain-swollen Tishomingo Creek and the men were forced to climb over the wreckage. In their frantic effort to escape, soldiers pushed comrades aside. Others, seeing it was hopeless to cross the bridge, attempted to wade or swim the creek. Many were drowned or shot as they floundered in the water.

On reaching the bridge, Forrest's men cleared it by pushing the wagons and the dead and wounded teams into the creek. Meanwhile, Forrest's escort forded the stream about 400 yards south of the bridge and bore down on the flank of the panic-stricken Federals. A number of prisoners were taken, along with some wagons. Although the sun was about to set, Forrest brought up his horse soldiers and personally took charge of the pursuit. A mile beyond the bridge, some of Sturgis' infantry rallied, but Captain Morton brought up two guns and smashed this pocket of resistance.

Throughout the night Forrest pressed the pursuit relentlessly. The morning of June 11 found the Federals passing through Ripley, 22 miles from Brices Cross Roads. Here Sturgis attempted to re-form his command. But the Confederates came up too soon, and the retreat was resumed. Not until he reached Salem at dark did

Forrest call off the chase. Sturgis' column, which had taken 10 days to reach Brices Cross Roads, retreated to Memphis in 64 hours. Union casualties in the fight and retreat were 2,612. Forrest listed his losses at 493 killed and wounded. The Confederates captured 250 wagons and ambulances, 18 cannon, thousands of stands of arms and rounds of ammunition, as well as the Federals' baggage and supplies.

A noted British soldier, Field Marshal, Viscount Wolseley, in commenting on Forrest's victory, called it

a most remarkable achievement, well worth attention by the military student. He pursued the enemy from the battle for nigh sixty miles, killing numbers all the way. The battle and his long pursuit were all accomplished in the space of thirty hours. When another Federal General was dispatched to try what he could do against this terrible Southerner, the defeated Sturgis was overheard repeating to himself . . . "It can't be done, sir: it c-a-n-t be done!" Asked what he meant, the reply was, "They c'-a-n-'t whip old Forrest!"

The disaster at Brices Cross Roads had important repercussions on Union strategy in the West. In early June 1864, plans had been made for a joint Army-Navy attack on Mobile, Ala., Adm. David G. Farragut already was strengthening his fleet blockading the entrance to Mobile Bay, and Gen. Edward R. S. Canby, commanding the Military Division of Western Mississippi, was concentrating a powerful army at New Orleans to be sent ashore at Pascagoula, Miss., and from there to strike overland at Mobile. To insure the success of his campaign, Canby counted on Gen. Andrew J. Smith and his two combat-tested infantry divisions.

After participating in the Red River Campaign in the spring, Smith and his veterans had started up the Mississippi River to reinforce Shermān in Georgia. Canby, however, convinced Sherman that Smith's corps should join him, and Smith was ordered to halt his troops at Memphis, preparatory to proceeding to New Orleans. Besides the force he was concentrating at New Orleans, Canby was massing several thousand cavalry near Baton Rouge. These horse soldiers were to strike eastward through southern Mississippi and cut the Mobile & Ohio Railroad.

Before Canby could complete his dispositions, word of Sturgis' defeat at Brices Cross Roads reached Union headquarters. Sherman fumed. He feared that Forrest would now advance into Middle Tennessee and destroy the railroad over which his armies received supplies and reinforcements. He would have to send another column into northeast Mississippi to seek out and destroy Forrest's cavalry corps. This force would be led by an officer in whom Sherman had confidence—A. J. Smith. Canby would have to forgo, at least for the time being, his attack on Mobile.

e line officers and soldirs deserve lasting ise for the manner in ich they endured the ships and fatigues of campaign; marching lusty roads with only e-half or one-third ons, under a broiling , with little water, is ainly a severe test of zeal and patriotism. honor be to the noble vhose breasts are the varks of our nation."

Gen. Andrew J. Smith

Smith, a Pennsylvanian, had graduated from the U.S. Military Academy in 1838. An "old army" man, he had served as Gen. Henry W. Halleck's chief of cavalry in 1862. Prior to the Red River Campaign, in which he had helped save the Union army from disaster, he had commanded a division at Chickasaw Bayou and in Grant's Vicksburg Campaign. Cautious and methodical, Smith was unlikely to let himself be trapped by Forrest.

Before taking the field, Smith saw that the railroad linking Memphis and La Grange was put back in operation. On June 22 he began shuttling his infantry into camps in and around La Grange. Here he was joined by General Grierson and his cavalry. The troops remained on the railroad until July 5, while Smith and his generals brought up supplies and perfected their plans.

Meanwhile, General Sherman had learned that the Confederates were rebuilding the railroad bridge across the Pearl River at Jackson, Miss. Fearing that they would use this line to reinforce Forrest in northeast Mississippi, he ordered Gen. Henry Slocum, commanding at Vicksburg, to send a column to Jackson to keep the Confederates from repairing the railroad. Slocum occupied Jackson on July 5 and during the next 3 days his troops engaged two Confederate brigades near the town. In these bloody fights, the Federals suffered the heavier losses, but Sherman's strategy paid off—Forrest received no reinforcements from this area.

In the meantime, a Federal amphibious force from Vicksburg had also been sent down the Mississippi and had gone ashore at Rodney. The Northerners drove inland and on July 5 engaged another Confederate brigade in a battle at Coleman's Plantation. Again the Northerners had the worst of the fighting, but more Confederate troops were pinned down.

Andrew J. Smith. Sm hardbitten, brusque, y popular with his men respected by his super Smith was a corps co mander temporarily d tached from the Uni Army of the Tennesse Sherman ordered him pursue Forrest on f devastating the land c which he passed or m pass, and make him a the people of Tennes and Mississippi real that, although a bold, ing, and successful lee he will bring ruin a misery on any coun where he may pause tarry."

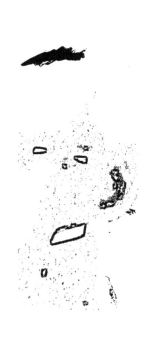

Late on the afternoon of July 5, about the same time that Slocum's troops were occupying Jackson and while the fight at Coleman's Plantation was at its height, Smith's 14,000 men and 24 cannon took the field. Two days later, they closed in on Ripley and encountered a roadblock defended by two of Forrest's regiments. The Confederates were brushed aside, and Smith's army felt its way slowly and cautiously down the Pontotoc Ridge, halting on the evening of July 9 at New Albany. The weather was hot, the roads were dusty, and water was scarce. Many units straggled badly. Although the infantry had not seen any more Confederates, the officers urged their men to be alert and keep a close watch on "the wagon train, the white canvas covers having always great attraction for Forrest's followers."

Forrest's command was given little opportunity to celebrate Sturgis' defeat. Even before the shattered Federal column reached safety, Confederate spies reported that Smith's troops had disembarked at Memphis. Forrest, headquartered at Tupelo, had maintained a close watch on Smith's activities and had kept Gen. S. D. Lee, informed on the Union buildup in and around La Grange. Lee decided to reinforce Forrest. Most of Gen. Philip D. Roddey's division was pulled out of north Alabama and rushed to Corinth and a mounted brigade joined Forrest from the Yazoo Country. The Confederate commander in southwest Mississippi started another brigade, but recalled it when Slocum advanced on Jackson. Five hundred heavy artillerists were issued riflemuskets and rushed northward by rail from Mobile. Cavalrymen with broken-down horses and mules were organized by Forrest into a dismounted division. The addition of these units increased the strength of Forrest's corps to 9,000 fighting men and 20 cannon.

Smith's army was only one of several Union forces threatening General Lee's department. His commander at Mobile warned that Admiral Farragut had strengthened his blockading squadron and that General Canby was massing troops at New Orleans; the Vicksburg Federals had taken Jackson; while on the Tennessee River in north Alabama a Union raiding column was being organized with its goal rumored to be the Selma arms factories. Forrest, himself, was suffering from boils.

On July 7, the day that Smith's vanguard broke the Confederate roadblock north of Ripley, S. D. Lee arrived at Forrest's headquarters. The two leaders decided to fortify a position covering Okolona, 18 miles south of Tupelo. There they would await attack, confident that Forrest's corps, fighting from behind earthworks, would maul Smith's infantry. Forrest would then counterattack with mounted infantry and destroy Smith's army.

To allow the Confederates time to throw up defenses and to bring Roddey's division down from Corinth, General Forrest, who would be in tactical command, sent several brigades up Ellistown Road to delay the advance of Smith's columns. On July 8, however, he discovered that his scouts had been fooled, and that the Federals were coming down the Pontotoc Ridge. Two more brigades were ordered to the front, and Gen. James R. Chalmers, as he rode forward, was told to delay the Northerners until the Confederates could complete their preparations to meet them. When Forrest gave the word, Chalmers was to retire to Okolona, and let Smith's army come on.

It took the Federals 2 days, July 10 and 11, to march from New Albany to Pontotoc, a distance of 20 miles.

Smith, to guard against disaster, moved his army whenever possible along parallel roads, so each column would be in easy supporting distance of the other. Large numbers of skirmishers covered the front, flanks, and rear. Smith's vanguard on both days clashed with Confederate detachments, while one of Forrest's patrols on the 11th threatened to sweep down on the rearguard.

Union soldiers on the evening of July 11 camped on the hills southeast of Pontotoc. Three of the roads leading south and east from Pontotoc were guarded by four of Forrest's brigades; Tupelo Road was patroled by a reinforced regiment. On the 12th, Smith rested his infantry, while General Grierson's cavalry scouted the roads.

An Illinois cavalry regiment, advancing down Okolona Stage Road, was mauled by Confederates. Information brought in by the cavalry satisfied General Smith that the Southerners had concentrated to the southeast of Pontotoc, leaving Tupelo unprotected. He accordingly ordered his division and brigade commanders to have their men ready to march for Tupelo at daybreak on July 13. If he could get there ahead of Forrest, he would not only secure a lodgment on the Mobile & Ohio Railroad, but he also would be able to choose his own ground and wait for the Confederates to attack him.

Unknown to Smith, other events were helping to insure the success of his plans. Slocum, after returning to Vicksburg from Jackson, had been reinforced and was now sweeping through the countryside between the Big Black and Bayou Pierre, while Farragut continued to add to his strength off Mobile Bay. Lee knew that he would have to bring Smith to battle soon or withdraw units from Forrest's corps for the defense of Mobile and southwest Mississippi. Chalmers was now ordered to fall back and let Smith come on. But when reports filtering into headquarters seemed to indicate (erroneously) that the Federals were about to withdraw, Lee counter-manded the order and, on the afternoon of the 12th, he and Forrest started for Pontotoc with the units they had assembled on the approaches to Okolona. They reached the front late that night.

As expected, much confusion resulted from the change in plans, and, on the morning of the 13th, when Smith started for Tupelo, the only Confederate force guarding the road was an understrength battalion which was brushed aside by an Iowa cavalry regiment. Early in the afternoon, Grierson's cavalry occupied Tupelo. Smith's infantry followed the horse soldiers. The wagon trains, as they rolled eastward, were well guarded. Colonel Bou-ton's black brigade watched the rear.

When the Confederates advanced they found the Union camps abandoned. Lee and Forrest realized what had happened. After a hurried discussion, Lee sent Forrest with a reinforced brigade to assail the rear of Smith's column; Lee himself would take the rest of the troops eastward, sending columns northward across Chiwapa Creek to strike the Federals in the flank. By attacking from two directions, he hoped to panic the Union infantry.

Forrest and his column pounded through Pontotoc. During the afternoon, he launched a number of attacks on the Union rearguard. The blacks more than held their own, as they parried Forrest's savage lunges. Sweeping across Chiwapa Creek, Col. Edward Rucker's brigade assailed one of Gen. Joseph Mower's infantry units as it was passing Burrow's shop. After destroying several wagons, Rucker's men were driven off. At Coonewah

Crossroads, 2 miles farther east, a fresh Confederate brigade charged toward the wagons and was routed by Mower's infantry. This defeat sapped the Southerners' vigor, and they made no further attempts to interfere with the march of Smith's infantry.

The day had gone extremely well for Smith, and if he and his officers congratulated themselves on the evening of the 13th, as their troops camped on the high ground west of Tupelo, they could be excused. They had stolen a march on Forrest and now held a strong position of their choosing. If the Confederates assaulted them here, they were confident that they could defeat them.

The Confederates camped for the night several miles west of Harrisburg. While the pickets took position, Forrest and an aide rode out to reconnoiter the Union lines. Although challenged and fired upon, they escaped after accomplishing their mission.

Generals Lee and Forrest held an early reveille on July 14. Covered by a strong force of skirmishers, the Confederates moved slowly forward. They had not gone very far when they encountered one of Grierson's mounted brigades that had ridden out Pontotoc Road to look for the enemy. Smith, on learning that the Confederates were advancing, called out his infantry. His battleline was on the crest of a low ridge and formed a right angle several hundred yards north of Pontotoc Road. To the front, the ground was open, sloping down to a small creek, beyond which the country was an undulating woodland with scant undergrowth but heavily timbered. From Smith's line, which was slightly more than 1½ miles long, the distance to the edge of the timber in front varied with the meanders of the branch. If the Confederates attacked, they would be exposed to artillery and

"Forrest seemed to know by instinct what was necessary to do. He was pleasant and companionable when he was not disturbed, but no occasion ever arose which he was not master of. He fought to kill but he treated his prisoners with all of the consideration in his power. So he did his own men. But he wanted the latter for service, and not merely to count."

Capt. James Dinkins,
Forrest's Cavalry Corps

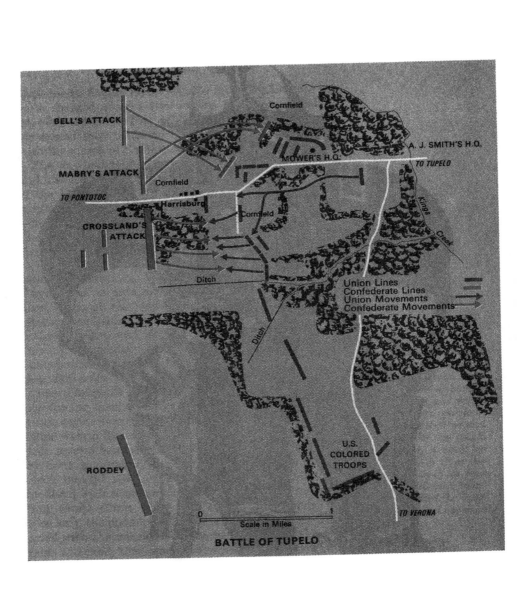

BELL'S ATTACK

Cornfield

MOWER'S H.Q.

A. J. SMITH'S H.Q.

TO TUPELO

MABRY'S ATTACK

TO PONTOTOC

Cornfield

Harrisburg

Cornfield

Kings Creek

CROSSLAND'S ATTACK

Ditch

Union Lines
Confederate Lines
Union Movements
Confederate Movements

Ditch

U.S. COLORED TROOPS

RODDEY

0   1
Scale in Miles

TO VERONA

BATTLE OF TUPELO

small-arms fire for distances varying from 300 to 1,000 yards. Several regiments strengthened their position by throwing up barricades of fence rails.

The Confederate leaders recognized the strength of the Union position, but Gen. S. D. Lee knew that Smith's force must be "dealt with vigorously and at once" so that he could redeploy his troops to reinforce the other portions of his department then under heavy pressure. After having decided to attack the Federals, Lee offered the command to Forrest, who declined. Lee answered, "If it is to be a fight, let us fight to the bitter end."

The Confederate battle plan was simple: it called for a frontal assault on Smith's position to cover Roddey's division as it swept around to envelop the Federal left. Forrest would be in charge of the flanking force.

While the brigade commanders were deploying their units, Confederate skirmishers drove in Grierson's horse soldiers, and the Confederate artillerists moved up 12 cannon and bombarded the Federals. Union gunners replied. Meanwhile, General Smith, sensing that the Confederates planned to turn his left, reinforced the troops holding that flank.

There were no clouds, and by 8 a.m. the day was already hot. Little rain had fallen during the past month and the ground was parched. The blades on the cornstalks were twisted, the leaves were withering, the roads were deep in dust, and many of the smaller streams had ceased to flow.

The three brigades Lee had marshaled north and south of Pontotoc Road attacked first. As the dismounted cavalrymen advanced, Col. Edward Crossland's Kentucky Brigade emerged from the timber and entered the cleared ground south of Harrisburg ahead of the other units. The Federals held their fire until the Kentuckians had closed to within 200 yards; then they opened "a most terrific fire of artillery and small-arms." The Kentuckians, despite heavy losses, pressed on; some of them were shot within 20 steps of Smith's battleline. The colors of the 12th Kentucky Cavalry were shredded; Col. W. W. Faulkner was wounded and his horse killed by an exploding shell, but he continued to advance until struck a second time. Seeing that the Southerners were starting to fall back, the Federals charged, sweeping the Kentuckians from the field. As they fled, some were heard to cry in despair, "My God! My God!"

Immediately after the defeat of Crossland's troops, Col. H. P. Mabry's brigade assailed the sector defended by Mower's division, north of the Pontotoc Road. Although suffering heavy losses, the Confederates lodged themselves within 70 yards of the Federals. Col. Tyree Bell's Tennesseans now came out of the timber and bore down on Mower's left. Crashing volleys, delivered point-blank, halted them, and they took cover in a hollow.

Meanwhile, Forrest was readying Roddey's division for a dash around the Union left. Seeing Crossland's brigade recoil in wild disorder, he recalled Roddey and rode to his left to rally the Kentuckians. The Confederate battle plan had now been ruined, and Lee called up Chalmers' division from the reserve. Chalmers, with Rucker's brigade, was rushed to the left. Storming forward, the brigade was mauled by Mower's bluecoats. Mower's division now counter-attacked and swept the three Confederate brigades from its front.

By 11 a.m. the Federals had won the battle. Four of the seven brigades committed by the Confederates had been smashed. Lee and Forrest had withdrawn to re-form their units while troops that had not been en-

"Soldiers! Amid you joicing do not forget gallant dead upon th fields of glory. Many noble comrade has f a costly sacrifice to country's independe The most you can do cherish their memor strive to make the fu as glorious as you they have made the

Gen. Nathan Bedford For

gaged were busy throwing up fortifications. Smith, however, did not press on to complete his victory and destroy
his opponents. Instead, he recalled Mower's troops, after
they had policed the field and brought in the wounded,
and had the soldiers strengthen their position.

The Confederates took advantage of this situation to
recover the initiative. About dark, they drove back
Union pickets near Harrisburg, while Forrest probed
Smith's left. To turn back these thrusts, Smith assembled a formidable force.

On the morning of July 15 Smith learned that rations
and ammunition were short, and he decided to return to
his base. The wagon train, escorted by one infantry division and a brigade of cavalry, started for La Grange via
Ellistown Road. Before Mower's division and the rearguard could move out, Forrest's horsemen dashed up
Verona Road and attacked the Union left. Once again,
they were repulsed.

Soon thereafter, Lee discovered that the Federals were
withdrawing from the area, and he placed Forrest in
charge of the pursuit. Two brigades overtook Smith's
rearguard before all the cavalry had crossed Oldtown
Creek. A four-gun battery opened fire, panicking the
horse soldiers, and Smith called for three infantry brigades to recross the stream. A desperate fight followed,
in which Forrest was wounded. With their popular general out of action, the Confederates, although reinforced,
were driven from the ridge commanding the Oldtown
Creek crossing.

The next day, Smith's column resumed its march. The
Confederates followed as far as the Tallahatchie, but
made no further attempts to harass the Federals. Smith's
return march in terrible heat, along dusty roads, on half-

rations, and with little water, was an ordeal which tested his soldiers' stamina. After an absence of 1 month, they were back in Memphis. Federal casualties in the campaign were 714 killed, wounded, or missing; the Confederates lost 1,326 killed and wounded, but made no report of their missing, which must have been numerous.

Like most Civil War operations, the Tupelo Campaign did not result in the destruction of either army. This campaign, along with the Battle of Brices Cross Roads and A. J. Smith's August expedition to Oxford, Miss., which triggered Forrest's raid on Memphis, was significant to the success of Sherman's Georgia Campaign. As Union armies inched closer to Atlanta, it became apparent that Sherman had failed in his goal to destroy the Confederate Army of Tennessee. Atlanta now became his primary objective, and a series of savage battles of attrition were fought on the approaches to that strategic city. In this fighting, the security of the single-track railroad over which Sherman supplied his armies was vital. Sherman therefore successfully employed columns operating out of Memphis to keep Forrest and his corps occupied in North Mississippi, hundreds of miles away from the Federal supply line. If Forrest had been allowed to raid into Middle Tennessee prior to the fall of Atlanta on September 2, it could have had disastrous consequences for the Union. Although Smith failed to destroy Forrest's corps at Tupelo on July 14, he did break its combat effectiveness. Forrest would rally his horsemen for more daring raids, but never again would they be able to fight and defeat infantry.

Brices Cross Roads National Battlefield Site and Tupelo National Battlefield are administered by the National Park Service, U.S. Department of the Interior. The Superintendent of Natchez Trace Parkway, whose address is Rural Route 5, NT-143, Tupelo, MS 38801, is in charge of both areas.

As the Nation's principal conservation agency, the Department of the Interior has basic responsibilities for water, fish, wildlife, mineral, land, park, and recreational resources. Indian and Territorial affairs are other major concerns of America's "Department of Natural Resources." The Department works to assure the wisest choice in managing all our resources so each will make its full contribution to a better United States—now and in the future.

National Park Service
George B. Hartzog, Jr., Director

United States Department of the Interior
Rogers C. B. Morton, Secretary

For sale by the Superintendent of Documents,
U.S. Government Printing Office
Washington, D.C. 20402 - Price 70 cents
Stock Number 2405-0285
★ U S GOVERNMENT PRINTING OFFICE 1972 O—452-381

CPSIA information can be obtained
at www.ICGtesting.com
Printed in the USA
BVHW05s1205020518
515050BV00020B/549/P